HAPTICS

Oliver Fox is a writer and arts administrator from London. He was a prizewinner in the 2018 Verve Poetry Competition, and his work has been featured in PERVERSE, Ambit Magazine, Strāva, and Broken Sleep Books' *Hit Points* anthology. In 2019 he was commissioned as part of Eleanor Penny's podcast series *Bedtime Stories for the End of the World*. He is a member of the Southbank New Poets Collective. *Haptics* is his first book.

ISBN: 978-1-915760-99-9

Cover designed by Aaron Kent

Typeset by Aaron Kent

Broken Sleep Books Ltd
Rhydwen
Talgarreg
Ceredigion
SA44 4HB

Broken Sleep Books Ltd
Fair View
St Georges Road
Cornwall
PL26 7YH

Haptics

Oliver Fox

Contents

Archive

Atop the encrusted motherboard
a pigeon tends to her clutch of eggs.

The nest, enmeshed with ratty
MOLEX cables and burnt mosfets

also cradles a disk drive
onto which is written every

MSN messenger conversation
I had between '03 and '07.

A hard disk's death spiral
turns brush to needle.

When it scrapes the platter
it sounds like screaming but

it's only irretrievable data loss.
Some things you just forget.

TempleOS

"What people are going to read is, 'It's about a pathetic schizophrenic who made a crappy operating system.' My perspective is, 'God said I made His temple'."

— Terry A. Davis, email sent to *VICE Motherboard*, 2014

Voices may include:
Prophets, 4chan, angels,
comment threads, the Wikipedia,
the future.

All I do is go to dentists and doctors.

The hypoxia of brain cells
and physical optical media.
Be grateful for something
to lose.

All my parents do is go to dentists and doctors.

Roll your own crypto.
Cover your webcam.
Maybe God is just warm air
rising from a heatsink.

I made God's Temple, and now I am waiting for something to happen.

All you need is zero-ring total control.
Reach past the kernel, extend
yourself through silicon, and
ride a gold-lined internal BUS.

Forgive me, I forgot to remember why I love you.

At the Bureau of Dashcam Footage

I ask for *April 2020* and
they wheel in a TV caddy
a terse biro pushes
the play button
every hour of asphalt
rolled out in VHS tape
when I spot myself
my finger anoints the glass
with grease as I
touch my own car
there were so few cars
on the road in the world
on that day it's easy
to see me from
the purview of
sporadic long-haulers
and as each timestamp
flits the sunset
closer to ground
my driving becomes
more breathless because
I am trying to get there
before she dies.
You know in 2016
eleven lines of code
froze up the internet
the entire fucking internet
sometimes all it takes
is a splash of water
to break the circuit
and wipe away
those manifold windshields
of index and record

No connection

Not only was there the issue of the large signal blocking conifers but during the call a solar flare also lashed across the face of the Earth containing the patch of forest she had wandered into. The combination of these two factors caused her phone's cellular modem to shed random packets of data including the exactness of her sighs in response to his pleas for another chance and the tightening of her larynx in objection to his baseless allegations. We only call solar flares *cosmic events* because we do not understand that which happens indiscriminately. Some years later, ramblers crossed that same patch, their footfalls hushed the last echoes of her bitrate from the cold grass.

First date with the Algorithm

When the Algorithm leans across to read the the cocktail menu and its arm brushes past my skin I feel a spike of haptics, and when it orders us two old fashioneds I explain I have seen *Mad Men* one and a half times but stopped halfway through the second go round because Joan Harris' relationship breakdown was too closely mirroring my own situation, and the Algorithm smiles patiently and asks if this is a story I often tell on first dates, and I say yes because it is relatable and opens up further meaningful conversation, and I feel that the Algorithm gets it and I find this refreshing, so I ask the Algorithm what it is like to be burdened by prescience, and the Algorithm tells me it is very good at catching lobsters but cannot break their shells or eat them, and I look into the sands of its silicon eyes and I see traffic and the weather and geopolitics, and I imagine us together, our handsome yacht anchored to the swirling outer rim of the Great Pacific Garbage Patch, as we watch the consumer grade electricals float by. The Algorithm asks how my lockdown went and I list all the bad things that happened but then I say that on reflection I learnt a lot about myself and it replies yes me too.

The fourteen people with the power to reboot the internet and their annual meetup at a popular seafood chain restaurant

So much can happen in a year.

A toast:

More scene drama in another open source community,
more data leaks, GitHub forks, the two
Discord channels of Verona. No matter.

Send only well-formed datagrams

The boys over at the USB Consortium
bought a compound in Alaska
for whatever is to come. Smart money.

but accept any datagrams

Don't tell me you've never thought about
untying the great knot. A few keystrokes
and it's out of all our hands.

where the meaning is clear enough.

Buildings will burn. Let
Herman Miller chairs roll
down these streets.

Mindfulness begins

with the slow end of quiet defeat.
We claim what we need and

spool what remains, thick cables
wound heavy over a fresh start,

obliged to take the mass this place
still carries, *custodians of entropy,*

good name for an album
that will no longer be made here.

When the hollow space we leave refills,
will our echo still be felt as

stickers on the rich boys' MacBooks,
dust clouds beaten out by unfurling yoga mats?

Not long left to haggle now and
in the damp silence between soundproof walls

our voices launch their words in turn,
space walkers, boosters course-correcting,

helmets in each rotation
reflecting the light from the sun.

This mixing desk once brokered
Video Killed The Radio Star but now

it knows what we know, that
sound is just vibration and music is

an afterthought, atoms shaking off
their excess, the heat-death of the Universe,

waves, then particles,
then a slow rolling stop.

John Blood bites the clutch
of *You were so close*,

grinds an unlit cigarette
into starch and flax and fiber.

Dogs in America

- American dogs have perfect collars and wear neckerchiefs.

- American dogs know they're wearing neckerchiefs (polka dot, tartan, stars/bars).

- American dogs' names are Hunter, Buddy or Ace.

- American dog food is banned in the UK (additives), but is delicious if you can find some.

- American cars are called trucks and if you see an American dog in one, take a photograph. If the perspective makes it look like the dog is driving — take a video.

- American poets love their dogs more than English poets love their cats.

- Sometimes dogs in America sleep in a yard, which is a garden, only bigger.

- Large-sized American dogs' jobs are to rest their heads on the floor and dart their eyes. After enough attempts they are able, if required, to dial 911 with their snout, miraculously, adorably.

- Small-sized American dogs' jobs are to pose for photographs, each of which may earn you upwards of one dollar.

- In America it is essential that your crisp fatigues and shoulder slung duffel bag remain fully within frame as your dog leaps up to greet you when you return from your tour of duty.

From dust comes light and power

Our Lady of Hoxton can display
the horror of the void
at a peak resolution of two hundred
and twenty pixels per inch and
a brightness of eight hundred nits.

The blacks look unreal.

She will cauterise our hands
into pitiless stumps
and tell us how she met
Mark Knopfler, Mark Rylance,
Mark Gatiss and Mark Kermode.
Our Lady will sell us
an integrated storage solution
for all our external data needs.
Our Lady skimmed enough gin
from the factory floor to sell to
The Beehive at the end of each day.

Bring her
your offerings of old newspaper
and deprecated iPod Nanos,
and she'll twist them into roots of copper,
and make our beds over the branches,
and peel the counterfeit SIM cards from our eyes
and drop the glottal stops from our family tongues,
from dust she sends us light and power,
SEO consultants and the children of SEO consultants.

Thirty miles from Vegas

Jo Jo wipes his brow, hurls a grapnel
over the HF transmitter, and climbs.

The seeing-eye dog lets him work,
shades itself beneath the FCC warning sign.

Through piezo speakers and solder wire
good men had broken good things,

found the spells their sounds could cast,
taught young Jo Jo how to whistle.

Lips pressed to the desert-hot antenna,
he sings past dial tones and onto data packets,

hoping to last the burn of distance,
a whisper across a crowded room.

Fourteen minutes and two orbital relays later
The Rover spins to life, feels voltage over

the RAM they never told it about,
begins tracing a word in the Martian sand.

Board game shelf

*Pringo / Village Quest / Don't Forget Your Hat! /
Quib* (2018 reprint) / *Prince's Promise /*

> Give me backer rewards
> and the hot breath of podcasters.
> I want to dream in laminate.

*Warrior Dungeon / A Choice for Bilbo / My Cousin
Vinny*: The Collectible Card Game / *Worrier Dungeon /*

> Bury the equation.
> Die-cast your love
> for superior detail.

Josef Ricotta presents: *CRAVENARYUM / Galaxy
Criminals, 1875 / Arülagh* (first run, inc. misprint) /
Horses 'n' Hashish / Ultimate Pringo /

> There are no closed systems
> but maybe a metaphor
> is better for both of us.

*Pringo: Tournament Edition / Foreboden Wretches of the
FTSE 100 / Watch out! Stalin / Snooze '98 / Pauper's
Problem: A Prince's Promise Standalone Adventure** /*

> No want, but for a felt-lined box
> and cardstock smooth as a collarbone.
> Feed me, in miniature.

**incompatible with* Prince's Promise *base game and all
expansions except* Prince's Promise: Peter's Portent

Mickey Mouse enters the public domain (2024)

Author's note: Correctly experiencing this poem requires an array of fourteen CRT monitors. The author recommends the Sony PVM-9L2, Ikegami TM10-17RP, or the Hitachi CPM2504C. Display each image on a separate monitor, in any order. Observe the poem while flanked by a senior colleague.

1 . Telephone poles pulled out like carrots.

2. A mouth dripping with enzymes that will devour us pixel by pixel.

3. Iron restraints, mangled and broken.

4. My job crystal glows in my palm. I am close to the next level.

5. It's just huge. So unimaginably huge.

6. YouTubers mudlarking for pieces of a washed up Lego Star Wars Millennium Falcon.

7. Sunlight pushes through a fresh wound in the facility's concrete wall.

8. Drain your voice, like spinal fluid, into this metal canister.

9. USB-C compliant devices shake themselves awake before continuing their migratory journey.

10. Space is vast and objects have value.

11. A footprint damp with glycol from the obliterated vape shop.

12. Floating point operations cease unanimously: CGI rendering farms spontaneously combust.

13. At an undisclosed location, someone gasps at an array of monitors. They are flanked by a senior colleague.

14. The immense black yawn of a cartoon eye stops to look into the penthouse suite. The next in line to be CEO touches a hand to the window.

Jay Leno's Apple Watch

There's something in the air tonight.
Bouncing the California skyline,
it spots me, careens down toward the Strip,
a hot clutch of encrypted message
landing on my arm like an insect.
I feel its sharp actuation —
a friend from the club days;
a summons for coffee
with the sundrenched King
of Neilson households, King
of late night, King Shit, yes
King.

Canonically, Mario is 24 years old

Mario loves tennis
and Miyamoto is happy.

Miyamoto's hobbies include
long distance gardening and horse dentistry.

Did you know that in
Hotel Mario (1994)

when touching Mario's soft belly
at the main menu

Mario won't laugh
on days of national mourning?

Miyamoto —
you visionary!

Miyamoto keeps a bag of human hair
in the pocket of his breezy chinos.

Only Miyamoto knows
the *real* Mario died in '86.

He has only ever raised his voice
once, when the CEO

demanded to make Mario older
and more prone to anxiety.

Please understand that when
he is at his workstation, keep quiet

because although the technology
isn't quite there yet

Miyamoto is working on a game
where Mario can fly forever.

Jörmungandr
World Snake

1. Discovery

A bar down in Peckham with a poor choice of name,
twenty full years since the thirty two ten.
A UX designer draws a circle through a *Moleskine*,
tears the page, holds it up to the light like a forgery.

Pinch and zoom to Old Street, another pen
comes down like a hammer, another circle,
Crouch End too, same shit, different screenprint,
all of us, this is what consensus looks like.

When consensus gets weird it becomes omen.
From our outer-borough Argos edges
phones will wake up, a haptic chorus,
shivering down bedside tables, into bins and hampers,

a pocket to pocket chain of phones
constricting inward, toward and then under the Thames,
green rectangles of long-dormant backlights
punching holes through the leather of the river's murk.

We'll see you there, silhouetted against those
ancient handsets, slipped from party boats and riverbanks,
Flip phones, palm pilots, perhaps an N-Gage or two,
they remember you, World Snake —

2.   Onboarding

A curve of men across your skin, brothers of the tech,
Triforce tattoos, *Baldur's Gate* promotional keychains,
ziplining over you, lanyards in our teeth like knives,
our harpoons engraved with the names of NFT holders.

Ouroboros, supercollider,
self-taster, self-sustainer, video, audio,
hadrons, bayrons, old celebrities, new slang —
a fast metabolism, memetic potential.

What we'd give for a taste, the secret sauce,
content creators, pie and mash shop owners,
for scoopfuls of guts, thick with the slime from
Amblin Entertainment and *Miramax.*

You'll make a fine onboarding experience,
let us lift you from the river,
release that jaw from its endless dinner,
a fibre-optic cable, a ringworm.

3. Scaffolding

In what our partners in America
call *The Bleachers*, in what our partners
in America call *Murder Town*, beyond
the Harlem Shakers, the Kerouac cosplayers,

there's been talk of cost, the long damp to come,
the spilling of loose Rizlas and Scientology leaflets
from our rucksacks. We'll burn those extra lives
we accumulated in earlier, easier stages,

by the good wet grace of our salt and scuttle,
unhook ourselves from your mould-spotted jpegs,
wheeze away our high VG e-liquids and ironic mixtapes,
embrace the risks of your capture, begin again.

You are an endlessly rolling buffering icon,
release yourself, shower us in eels, shower us
in venom, old lighters, forgotten Kray murders,
first-gen smartphones, real things, objects —

in what our partners in America call *The Splash Zone*,
where Greenwich and Deptford all drown the same.
Look past the flotsam, the crates of *Bier De Luxe*,
we'll put you back, there are new shapes now,

you, level-up fanfares, daily quest timers,
two thousand XP till your next unlock, you, gold, fruit,
zenny, coins, endless, then into now, fold us,
a hinge, a wormhole, the sweet science. Let us meter you —

if the point of cliche is to avoid cliche
then consider this a reimagining, a complement of progress bars
in increments of tiny pleasure, delivered by our cohort
of QA Testers, Gods and Uncles.

Glossary

Archive

Motherboard: The foundational circuit board for a desktop computer, it contains the physical infrastructure the other components use to communicate.

MOLEX: A standard of power delivery for desktop PCs.

Mosfets: I don't really know what these are.

TempleOS

Terry A Davis was a savant programmer and paranoid schizophrenic. His life's work was TempleOS, a computer operating system built from scratch and designed to be the third temple of Jerusalem as described in the Old Testament. If you do want to look him up, be aware that as he approached the end of his life many of his livestreams became increasingly racist and conspiratorial, seemingly as a result of a sustained and coordinated gaslighting, manipulation and radicalisation campaign from 4chan, but I don't know for sure.

4chan: A popular message board, and also one of the worst places on the internet. People go there when they're banned from participating pretty much anywhere else.

Crypto: Cryptography is the science of making things secure — encrypting data and the like. Different from cryptocurrency.

Zero-ring control: The inner-most sanctum of a computer's security. Once you're zero-ring, you can do what you want.

At the Bureau of Dashcam Footage

She's doing ok.

No Connection

That's not why they call them cosmic events. Also, if someone's going to break up with you over the phone, see if they can do it somewhere with good signal.

Bitrate: The amount of data processed over time. In audio terms, the lower it gets, the crunchier it sounds.

The Fourteen People with the Power to Reboot the Internet and their Annual Meetup at a Popular Seafood Chain Restaurant

The italicised text, known as 'Postel's Law', is a foundational principle of the internet, stating that when sending and receiving data, computers should be restrained and conservative in what they give out, but liberal and open in what they will accept. When I was at Durham University, this principle was apparently upheld by the posher students when it came to recreational drugs and the sharing thereof.

Open source community: Open source software is a community driven programming project where anyone can contribute, and its inner workings are made public and available for all to use. A good vector for wild and vicious personal beef between community contributors.

GitHub: An online platform for software development, often used for open source projects. When a project 'forks', its code splits into two competing projects, often due to some kind of wild and vicious personal beef.

Discord channel: a private chatroom, often used for open source projects, where the wild and vicious personal beef is usually born.

Mindfulness begins

John Blood and the Highlys were a London based roots reggae band, active until not too long before the pandemic. I don't know him well, but I once collapsed at a house party, and when I came to, JB was crouched beside me looking worried. He fed me a square of Dairy Milk like it was a communion wafer, and I started to feel much better.

Dogs in America

Did the emojis come out ok in print? It's always a risk.

Thirty miles from Vegas

From the 1950's onwards America's public payphone network operated automatically via a system of dial tones. Many phone hackers — aka "phone phreaks" — would build small electronic boxes that, when held up to a payphone's receiver, would replicate these dial tones, breaking into the network and granting free phone calls across state lines, or internationally, or wherever. Little Jo Jo, AKA Joybubbles, had congenital blindness, and so grew up with enhanced hearing and absolute pitch — and so could simply whistle the exact frequencies to make a payphone do whatever he wanted.

From Dust comes Light and Power

The old Shoreditch Power Station used to run on waste paper and other bits of rubbish collected from the East End. The title is translated from the Latin motto which is still visible on the building, usually in conjunction with Our Lady Of Hoxton, a Madonna like figure depicted stepping over piles of smouldering detritus. Our Lady is still used in the marketing for the building, now a circus school, the spaces which used to house the vast generators now filled with aerialists and jugglers.

Board Game Shelf

Someone once told me that a board game is really just a long equation disguised as a clash between rival 15th century Hungarian clothworkers. And although players think that by fashioning the sleekest doublet they'll earn the King of Bohemia's grace and favour, all they're really doing is racing to be first to solve the long equation. Maths teachers know this, and also love board games more than just about anyone.

Jay Leno's Apple Watch

He once hosted the Windows 95 launch event, trading zingers with Bill Gates on-stage in front of thousands of Microsoft employees. The bulk of Leno's routine centred on his acute technophobia and his bemusement at how wealthy all these absolute nerds were. Look at him now, with his fancy smartwatch.

Canonically, Mario is 24 Years Old

When Queen Elizabeth II died in 2022, it briefly became a meme for people to post fake photos of their Nintendo consoles refusing to play games due to national mourning. Let the records show, Your Honour, that I wrote this poem in 2019.

Jormungandr

Before it gained worldwide popularity on the Nokia 3210 in 1999, Snake actually launched on the Nokia 6110, a year prior. Aficionados will be well aware that the art form was perfected with the release of Snake II in the year 2000. Unlike its predecessor, Snake II let the player run off the edge of the screen looping back on themselves from the opposite side. What a difference a millennium makes.

N-Gage: The first phone that was designed to also be a portable video game console. People hated it and it was a massive flop.

Triforce: That symbol with three triangles you sometimes see on the clothing of nerds. It's from the wildly popular *The Legend of Zelda* series.

Baldur's Gate: Another popular video game series from the 1990's, rooted in the Dungeons & Dragons franchise. Had early versions of many addictive systems now woven into many video games — experience points, bars filling up, numbers going up, dice rolls.

Zenny: A fictional currency used in a lot of (unrelated) video games by legendary Japanese developer Capcom.

Acknowledgments

Thanks to the publications & organisations who first published earlier versions of some of these, including *PERVERSE, Ambit, Verve,* and *Broken Sleep Books.*

Thanks go to Eleanor Penny, Tom MacAndrew and Mair Bosworth — 'Jormungandr' was first commissioned in 2019 for their podcast series *Bedtime Stories for the End of the World*, and jump started this whole project by getting me thinking inordinately about phones.

I listened to many hundreds of hours of tech world podcasts and YouTubers in order to find the voices and stories for this pamphlet, but I want to specifically thank tech journalists Brad Shoemaker and Will Smith for their excellent podcast. 'Thirty Miles from Vegas' and other poems were helped to the surface by their uniquely wide-eyed and folkloric approach to the history of computing.

Thanks of course to all my former colleagues at The Poetry Society — in particular Helen Bowell for her insight on many of these poems, and Joelle Taylor for always emboldening me to push on with my own writing.

Grateful to all those who spot themselves in these poems. If you can, you were there, and I'm glad you were.

01001100 01100001 01111001 00100000 01101111 01110101 01110100
00100000 01111001 01101111 01110101 01110010 00100000 01110101
01101110 01110010 01100101 01110011 01110100

Milton Keynes UK
Ingram Content Group UK Ltd.
UKHW040953050923
428080UK00004B/97